HURRICANE IAN

Everything you should know about hurricanes, with respect to Ian.

By

Dr. Elba D. Tyler

Copyright© 2022 by Dr. Elba D. Tyler

TABLE OF CONTENTS

<u>**INTRODUCTION**</u>

One of nature's most potent storms is the hurricane. They cause tornadoes, rip currents, and inland floods by way of strong winds, storm surge inundation, and heavy rainfall.

Hurricanes also referred to as tropical cyclones, are low-pressure systems that develop over tropical or subtropical oceans and feature organized thunderstorm activity. The warm ocean waves provide them with energy.

A hurricane is a storm with sustained winds of at least 74 mph that gathers strength as it passes over warm ocean water. In the warm regions of the Atlantic, Pacific, and Gulf of Mexico oceans, hurricanes arise.

Tropical storms are large storms that develop from warm ocean water but do not attain sustained wind speeds of at least 74 mph.

The American hurricane season runs from June 1 to November 30. Warm ocean waters are present during this time, and moisture evaporates and rises into the atmosphere. As a result of the rising air, a low-pressure area is formed, attracting winds from the regions nearby. The winds spiral upward as a result of the warm, humid air warming them. The whirling quickens, producing the hurricane.

HURRICANE CATEGORIES

Utilizing a scale from one to five, the Saffir-Simpson Hurricane Wind Scale is used to classify hurricanes. A significant hurricane can do more total damage than a tropical storm or a category one or two hurricanes.

In the Atlantic Ocean, the Gulf of Mexico, and the Eastern Pacific Ocean, hurricanes begin to intensify in the warm tropical waters.
From June 1 to November 30 is hurricane season in the Atlantic Ocean. The hurricane season runs from May 15 to November 30, but hurricanes that affect the Eastern Pacific region may appear earlier.

The weakest hurricane is classified as Category 1. The sustained winds of a Category 1 storm range from 74 to 95 mph.

The storm will only cause minor damage to the coastline despite having winds that are faster than the cheetah, which is the fastest animal on Earth.

The sustained winds of a Category 2 hurricane range from 96 to 110 mph. This is comparable to a pitcher's greatest fastball in Major League Baseball.

A professional tennis player's greatest service is comparable to the sustained winds of a Category 3 hurricane, which range from 111 to 130 mph.

A Category 4 hurricane can reach sustained winds of up to 155 mph, which is faster than the fastest rollercoaster in the world.

Additionally, a Category 5 storm has sustained winds of more than 155 mph. With gusts as swift as some of the world's fastest high-speed trains, category 5 hurricanes can cause the most devastating devastation.

DESCRIPTION OF DAMAGES

Category 1

- There is now extremely unsafe wind speed.
- Even in well-built homes, damage to the roof and shingles is a possibility.
- Houses' vinyl gutters and siding could be harmed.
- Homes with substandard construction or mobile homes would have been significantly damaged
- Small trees or trees with weak root systems are more likely to topple.
- Enormous trees may break their large branches.
- Significant damage to electricity lines might result in days-long power outages.

Category 2

- The wind is now moving at a very frightening rate.
- Homes with solid construction could sustain significant gutter, vinyl siding, and roof damage.
- Mobile dwellings and poorly built homes are likely to sustain significant damage.
- Large branches may break or several trees will be uprooted.
- Power outages are likely to be prolonged and extensive, lasting days or perhaps weeks.

Category 3

- Wind speeds have increased to the point of doing terrible harm.
- The roof ends and decks could sustain damage.

- Mobile homes and poorly built homes sustain significant damage.

- Large branches will fall off and uproot several trees.

- After the storm, it's possible that there won't be any access to water or electricity for days or perhaps weeks.

Category 4

- Rapid wind gusts can result in catastrophic destruction.

- Mobile dwellings and shoddy constructions will be torn down.

- Well-built homes' walls and roofs are susceptible to severe damage.

- There will be extensive tree uprooting of all sizes.

- The destruction of electrical poles and lines is possible.
- The area becomes briefly inhabitable when there are weeks or months of water and electricity outages.

Category 5

- will result in severe harm.
- Mobile homes and houses with shoddy construction will be destroyed.
- Many homes with sturdy frames will have their roofs and walls demolished.
- The majority of trees will be uprooted and damaged.
- For weeks or probably months, the area won't be habitable due to a lack of water and power.

<u>An explanation of a Category 5 hurricanes</u>

A Category 5 hurricane may maintain winds of 157 mph or more. A Category 5 storm is the most severe and causes catastrophic destruction.

We can better understand the devastation a Category 5 hurricane might cause by referencing the famous Great Galveston Hurricane of 1900. With between 8000 and 10,000 fatalities, this was the deadliest American incident ever.

An unusually large rise in the ocean level, known as a storm surge, is what led to the high death toll. Most of the time, a hurricane's storm surge causes the most damage.

A Category 5 hurricane also has the following effects:

- strong rains

- brisk breezes

- tree branches uprooted and electricity lines destroyed

- Complete mobile home destruction

- Most framed houses have had their walls and roofs destroyed.

- Tornadoes are small, on-land whirling winds.

- significant flooding brought on by the rain and storm surge

The surface winds are constantly circling as storm systems intensify into hurricanes. The direction of circulation varies depending on where the storm is located: it is counter-clockwise in the Northern hemisphere and clockwise in the Southern hemisphere. Meteorologists refer to this pattern as "closed circulation."

The hurricane's recognizable "eye," the calm, clear center of the storm, is formed by these rotating winds and is encircled by the eyewall, where winds are at their greatest.

The names of the three types of storms—hurricanes, typhoons, and cyclones—depend on where they originate.

These storms are known as "hurricanes" in the North Atlantic and the central and eastern North Pacific. Typhoons are what they are known as in the western North Pacific, and cyclones are what they are known as in the South Pacific and the Indian Ocean. (Tropical cyclones in the South Atlantic are uncommon.)

When a storm intensifies into a tropical storm, it is given a name. A global council of the World

Meteorological Organization offsite link selects the names (WMO). The WMO may withdraw the name of a storm that was extremely deadly or expensive, but names are typically renewed every six years.

Tropical Storm Allison in memory

We reflect on Tropical Storm Allison, which never reached hurricane strength but caused catastrophic floods in portions of Texas, on its 18th anniversary.

What causes tropical storms to form?

An atmospheric disturbance, such as a tropical wave or cluster of thunderstorms, causes tropical storms to form.

These environmental factors must exist for these disturbances to develop into a tropical cyclone:

- Ocean waters that are warm (at least 80°F/27°C).

- an unstable environment caused by temperature variations, where the temperature drops with height.

- Near the middle of the atmosphere, moist air.

- It can only spin if it is at least 200 miles (rare instances excepted) north or south of the equator (due to the Coriolis effect).

- little variation in wind direction or speed with height (known as low vertical wind shear).

HURRICANE SAFETY

Numerous hazards to persons and property are posed by hurricanes, tropical storms, and tropical depressions. The two main causes of fatalities during storms historically have been storm surges and inland floods. Strong gusts, tornadoes, heavy surf, and rip currents can all be brought on by hurricanes. The best time to get ready for a hurricane is before it makes landfall, which in the Atlantic is on June 1, and in the Eastern and Central Pacific is on May 15.

Only a portion of the tale is revealed by hurricane categories.

The Saffir-Simpson Hurricane Wind Range, which rates wind speed on a scale from one to five, is used to classify hurricanes.

A significant hurricane can do more total damage than a tropical storm or a category one or two hurricanes.

Hurricane wind scale Saffir-Simpson

Herb Saffir, a wind engineer, and Bob Simpson, a meteorologist, developed the scale to help explain the damage that buildings may endure at various wind speeds. It's important to note that the Saffir-Simpson scale does not take storm surges, floods, or rain threats into account.

Each storm is unique.

Each tropical system has its own distinct set of potentially fatal risks that it might bring to a specific area. Knowing your risk is essential, especially if you reside in a storm surge evacuation zone or a potential flood zone.

Even if you've already weathered a storm in your region, subsequent hurricanes could present new dangers.

Before watches or warnings are issued for your area for storms or storm surges, local officials may issue evacuation orders. To provide inhabitants adequate time to evacuate susceptible regions before the first storm threats appear, evacuation orders are issued. When ordered, be ready to leave and do so without delay.

Hurricanes provide heavy rainfall.

Compared to chilly air, warm air can hold more moisture. The air is especially warm and can hold a lot of moisture during tropical cyclones. Much more frequently than with a regular low-pressure system remote link, the moisture cools as it rises and condenses into heavy rain.

These rains can fall kilometers inland as well as on the shore, resulting in floods that can last for days or even weeks after a storm. Always heed evacuation warnings, and avoid driving through flooded areas. Always have an evacuation strategy in place before a storm hits if you reside in a low-lying or prone to flooding location.

The current status of hurricane forecasting

The National Hurricane Center has a lengthy history of giving tropical cyclone advisories, with the first forecast for a tropical cyclone being made in 1954 and being logged for 24 hours. Since then, forecasts have included predictions of intensity, size, and related hazards like wind, storm surge, and rainfall. They have also been extended in time.

The largest danger comes from water, not wind.

Hurricane storm surge poses the biggest threat, although their powerful and destructive winds are well known.

Water that is pushed toward the beach by winds spinning around the storm is known as a storm surge. In coastal places, this surge in sea level could result in catastrophic disaster. The threat from storm surges is enormous since a large portion of the highly populated Atlantic and Gulf Coast coastlines of the United States are less than 10 feet above mean sea level. Storm surge has historically been responsible for nearly half of the direct deaths caused by storms that make landfall in the United States. Always heed the call to evacuate.

Run from the water and take cover from the wind.

When you're at risk of flooding, you should move to the high ground far from water and any regions that are prone to flooding. When there are strong gusts but no risk of flooding (unusual in hurricanes but crucial during any storm), it's crucial to take cover inside a sturdy building far from doors and windows.

Due to this, wind-related evacuation orders are rarer than water-related ones.

After a storm has passed, be cautious!

When the weather clears, hurricane-related risks remain. Use generators responsibly after the storm, take care not to overdo it, and wait until it is safe to enter storm-damaged areas.

After storms pass, numerous fatalities are reported as a result of heart attacks, problems with power outages, and accidents.

Educational Connection

Hurricane impacts alter along with climate change. Communities along the coast are especially at risk because storm surge flooding is made worse by increasing sea levels.

With the help of this collection, teachers and students may learn about how storms develop, potential repercussions, hurricane preparation, and even a citizen science project that uses satellite imagery to categorize hurricanes.

HURRICANE IAN

As a storm passes through Florida, cities are inundated and lose power.

2.4 million homes and businesses in Florida are without power as a result of one of the most severe storms to batter the US in recent memory, and flooding is rushing inland.

On Wednesday at 15:10 local time (19:10 GMT), Hurricane Ian made landfall, slamming into the coast with winds as high as 241km/h (150mph).

Dramatic scenes included trees being uprooted, a hospital roof being blown off, and cars being submerged. Later, the hurricane's category four status was lowered to a tropical storm.

But Florida residents were forewarned that the most hazardous 24 hours were still to come.

Tampa's mayor asked residents to remain indoors through the night and into Thursday early.

The Weather Prediction Center warned Central Florida Peninsula residents to expect "widespread life-threatening, catastrophic flash and urban floods" to last until Friday AM with local rainfall reaching up to 76cm (30ins).

Although residents were told to leave their houses, many chose to stay and seek safety inside.

Live:

- Two million loose power as a result of Hurricane Ian
- After a storm, Cuba starts to restore power.
- Living in Venice, about 60 miles (95 kilometers) south of Tampa, Mark Pritchett described the "terrifying" moment he stepped

outside of his house as the hurricane moved across the Gulf of Mexico.

- "Raindrops that shoot like needles The water in my street "He stated this to the Associated Press news organization through text message.

- Healthcare staff at HCA Florida Fawcett Hospital in Port Charlotte, which is a little bit further south, were forced to remove their most fragile patients from the intensive care unit when the roof was torn off.

- Due to storm damage, police were unable to respond to reports of looting at a gas station in Lee County, where Ian made landfall in the southwest.

- As a result, a curfew has been put in place and will be in effect "until further notice".

- The community of Fort Myers has "been somewhat destroyed," according to Lee County Manager Roger Desjarlais.

- Some of the 80,000-person city's neighborhoods have been left to resemble lakes, according to the news agency AFP.

- Ron DeSantis, the state governor, called Ian the "largest flood disaster" southwest Florida had ever seen and declared that 7,000 National Guard soldiers are prepared to spearhead rescue efforts.

After viewing "devastating" pictures of the damage inflicted by Ian, Vice President Kamala Harris advised Americans to heed evacuation instructions.

Ian is currently making its way across Florida as it travels north. North-east Florida's Jacksonville International Airport canceled every aircraft on Thursday.

By Thursday AM local time, the storm is anticipated to enter the Atlantic.

On Friday, it's anticipated to arrive in Georgia and South Carolina. Virginia has also proclaimed a state of emergency, joining Georgia, North Carolina, South Carolina, and Florida in doing so.

Hurricane Ian made landfall on Cuba's western coast on Tuesday. After the island went completely dark, power has recently been restored in certain sections. It is thought that two people were killed in Cuba and that over 20 Cuban migrants were traveling to the US and are missing at sea.

Damage descriptions of Hurricane Ian

In Jamaica, Ian proceeded to the south of the country, bringing with it swells, storm surge, and three to six inches of rain that impacted coastal areas. The flash flood warning was in place until the morning hours of September 26.

Localized flooding in some parishes, like Clarendon, led to the activation of emergency shelters. The tropical storm watch for Jamaica was lifted as Ian veered away from the island.

As a Category 1 Hurricane, Ian traveled southwest of the Cayman Islands, closing roads and docks due to flooding-related debris that restricted access points. Water system disruptions and power outages were recorded, but as of September 27, both services had nearly fully recovered.
Ian's erratic course presented difficulties for preparedness and reaction efforts.

After Hurricane Ian hit the US, at least 87 deaths have been verified, and rescuers are frantically looking for survivors among the wreckage of flooded homes.

Authorities in Florida and South Carolina are still evaluating the damage as one of the strongest and costliest hurricanes in American history moves north.

About 10,000 people are still missing, although police believe many are likely in shelters or without electricity, and Ian has been compared to an "A-bomb."

The announcement comes as First Lady Michelle Obama and Vice President Joe Biden declared their intention to visit Florida and Puerto Rico the following week to see the damage and meet with authorities and locals after the hurricane devastated both areas.

More than 1,300 disaster workers are assisting recovery operations across five states, according to the American Red Cross.

83 of those killed—mostly by drowning—occurred in Florida. However, the storm also had unintended consequences, as an elderly couple died when their oxygen devices stopped functioning as a result of a power outage.

Four further fatalities related to the extreme weather were recorded in North Carolina, two of whom were killed in a car accident that occurred during the storm.

Although Hurricane Ian has now been downgraded to a cyclone, officials have warned the storm is still dangerous. For most of the week, Hurricane Ian's winds and coastal surges have terrified millions of people.

According to the National Hurricane Center, the storm is presently moving away from southern Virginia.

As the scope of the destruction became apparent, it nevertheless left floods and power disruptions throughout the Carolinas.

Large portions of the east coast, including New York, New Jersey, and Washington, D.C., are still expected to see "treacherous" weather conditions this weekend.

The major clean-up operation is still underway in Florida, where the most recent data indicates that more than 1.1 million people still lack WiFi and electricity.

Elon Musk, the CEO of SpaceX, has reportedly agreed to make Starlink, the company's satellite internet service, available to anyone without connectivity who is attempting to contact loved ones or seek assistance.

Celebrities are starting to contribute to relief efforts as well.

Currently playing for the Florida-based Tampa Bay Buccaneers, American football legend Tom Brady tweeted that he will be making a donation to the Florida Disaster Fund and urged other NFL players to follow suit.

Ian pounded beachfront Georgetown on Friday with winds of 85 mph, just to the north of Charleston, the oldest city in South Carolina.

Four piers along the coast were partially destroyed by the hurricane, including two that were connected to the well-known tourist destination of Myrtle Beach. More than 63,000 households and businesses in the state still lacked electricity on Saturday.

The Federal Emergency Management Agency has been permitted to coordinate disaster relief efforts across the state's 100 counties and for the Eastern Band of Cherokee Indians, a federally recognized Indian tribe based in western North Carolina.

President Biden approved the emergency declaration for the region.

Residents of Cuba's capital city Havana have protested in the streets about the continued blackouts following its direct touchdown, 5 days ago.

A new weather storm is reportedly moving toward Mexico's northwest Pacific coast.

According to the US National Hurricane Center, Orlene had strengthened into a hurricane and was on track to make landfall early next week with gusts of 75 mph.

<u>Effects of hurricanes</u>

Strong winds and significant rainfall are also brought by a hurricane when it makes landfall. We already know that one of a hurricane's effects is wind and that wind speed is what permits us to classify storms. A hurricane's powerful winds have the potential to uproot trees, topple electrical lines, and harm structures.

Damages from hurricanes have increased significantly in recent years. The 1990s have already caused more damage than the 1970s and 1980s put together (even after adjusting for inflation). Each decade from the 1950s through the 1980s saw a decline in the number of hurricane-related fatalities, but by the middle of the 1990s, it seemed that this trend had stopped.

The Impact Assessment Challenge: Judging Damages

There is a desire for an exact dollar amount of damages in the wake of any extreme incident.

The expenses of a hurricane can be calculated in a variety of reliable methods. To make the estimate easier to grasp, assumptions driving the study must be made explicit in any assessment of consequences leading to an estimate of the overall damages associated with a disaster. Five elements that can derail damage assessment demand the analyst's attention: contingency, quantification, attribution, aggregation, and comparison.

The issue of multiple-order impacts is a contingency A hurricane's obvious path of damage is left behind when it hits a neighborhood.

Homes, businesses, and crops may be destroyed or damaged, as well as public infrastructure, and individuals may sustain injuries or lose their lives as a result of strong winds and storm surge water.

Due to the direct correlation between the incident and the damages, such clear effects are referred to as "direct impacts." Due to their distinct nature, direct impacts' costs are typically the simplest to calculate. Federal funding, the repair of public infrastructure, and the disposal of debris are all examples of indirect effects that may be measured.

A hurricane's indirect effects are referred to as secondary effects. Secondary effects typically manifest in the days and weeks after a hurricane has passed. As an illustration, a hurricane might demolish a water treatment facility (Changnon 1996). The cost of reconstructing the plant is the direct consequence; secondary effects could include the price of delivering fresh water to the community. Since they require estimation and are a result of an ongoing social process, such secondary effects are typically harder to measure.

For instance, calculating the costs of providing fresh water in place of what the plant would have provided requires some understanding of what would have happened in the absence of the hurricane's impact. Impacts of further order over timescales of months and years happen and are easily envisioned.

For instance, a cyclone might wipe out many local businesses, reducing visitor traffic and, consequently, the amount of sales tax collected. As a result, community services that had been supported by sales tax receipts may decline, resulting in more social unrest and expenses.

Due to multiple confounding factors, it is difficult to estimate the costs associated with such impacts with a high degree of confidence.

In summary, a hurricane operates as a shock to a community and has a variety of effects that have both short- and long-term effects on the social structure.

As the impact is further removed in time and causation from the event's direct impacts, it becomes harder to distinguish the signal of the reverberations from the noise of ongoing social processes.

Attribution: The Causation Problem

Contingency and attribution go hand in hand. People are quick to blame nature after a natural disaster: "The hurricane cost billions of dollars in damages." However, "natural" calamities frequently result from mistakes made by people. Instead of only being the product of nature's powerful forces, the damage is frequently the outcome of prior mistakes and a lack of planning.

Disasters frequently happen when unpreparedness, intense occurrences, and both collide.

Understanding what losses and damages would have been avoidable vs what losses and damages were unavoidable is a crucial part of learning from a catastrophe. Gross tabulations of damages frequently implicitly blame nature rather than ourselves and ignore the question of why the damage occurred.

Quantification: The Measuring Issue

What is the cost of a life? Or, to put it another way, how much public money are people willing to spend to rescue one more life from an environmental threat? Human life is valued by the public at between $2.0 million and $10.9 million, according to a study by Fischer et al. (1989).

The challenges involved in putting a monetary value on human life are an example of the more widespread issue with estimating many of the costs resulting from a hurricane's impact. What is the worth of a lost ecosystem, park, unrecoverable period in school, etc.? These are examples of similar queries. What are the expenses incurred as a result of psychological trauma? The challenges of putting a dollar figure on losses that are not primarily economic in origin are exemplified by the challenges of calculating the cost of a life.

Other societal effects of a hurricane are not directly related to economic factors (e.g., well-being). As a result, any thorough economic assessment of a hurricane's impact must include a calculation of the expenses related to subjective losses.

As a result, one's assumptions can have an impact on the final result when evaluating value.
It is important to be open about these assumptions throughout the analysis.

The Issue of Benefits and Spatial Scale in Aggregation

Hurricanes don't always cost money, but estimations of their effects rarely take advantages into account. Think about the following instance: Commodity prices increase nationally after a cyclone that significantly lowers agricultural productivity in a region. As a result, although farmers in the affected zone experience losses, farmers outside the area may benefit greatly from the hurricane. Thus, the hurricane can have positive net economic effects on the country.

The example of farmers experiencing advantages or losses based on their farming location highlights two types of problems: benefits and spatial scale.

Arguably, certain people and organizations get something positive from every calamity.

Should the impact of a hurricane be reduced to account for these benefits? Additionally, the scope of the analysis affects how much damage is shown.

For the same incident, a county may suffer destruction, the state may be affected moderately, and the country may profit. Wealth transfers through disaster relief exacerbate the situation. Since there are several legitimate spatial dimensions from which to view a hurricane's effects, it is important to pay close attention to the goals of damage estimations. Additionally, it's critical to keep in mind that repercussions extend beyond things that can be quantified in money; pain and suffering are losses regardless of size.

Comparison: The Demographic Change Issue

Comparing hurricane impacts through time and space is difficult due to the difficulties in conducting significant impact assessments.

If prior hurricanes had struck more recently, their lasting effects undoubtedly would have been stronger. However, damage statistics frequently only capture the occurrence and economic harm in the historical record (usually adjusted only for inflation). Such numbers can cause people to draw incorrect assumptions about the importance of storm damage trends.

Such numbers may vastly underestimate our susceptibility because the population and property at risk from hurricanes have changed significantly this century. As a result, caution must be exercised when concluding policy using bottom-line damage estimates.

The Verdict: Pairing oranges with oranges and apples with apples

The expenditures connected with a storm can be calculated in a variety of ways. There is no single, ideal method.

The method used to calculate the costs of damages must be set for each situation because it depends on the goals for which the calculation is being conducted.

Whatever approach is used, the analyst must be sure of at least two things when calculating or using the expenses related to a hurricane's impact. The analyst must first be clear about the assumptions that underpin the evaluation, including what is being measured, how it is being measured, and why. Second, contrast oranges and apples side by side.

When comparing the effects of a recent storm to those of a past hurricane or a hurricane to an earthquake, the methods used should lead to results that make sense in a comparative context.

<u>Economic losses, casualties, and hurricane frequency are all on the rise.</u>

After accounting for inflation, hurricanes alone caused an average annual loss of $1.6 billion in the United States from 1950 to 1989, $2.2 billion from 1950 to 1995, and $6.2 billion from 1989 to 1995. (Hebert et al. 1996).

For instance, from 1986 to 1994, typhoon-related damages in China were an average of $1.3 billion (unadjusted).

Other nations, including those in Southeast Asia, the Indian Ocean (including Australia), the Caribbean and Pacific islands, and Central America, have also suffered significant devastation from tropical cyclones (including Mexico).

Although a complete accounting of these damages has not yet been made public, it is safe to assume that they are in the billions of dollars, with a conservative estimate of $10 billion annually (1995 USD).

Other projections vary up to $15 billion each year (Southern 1992).

Over the years 1986 to 1995, 196 Americans perished as a result of hurricanes (Hebert et al. 1996). According to experts, tropical cyclones cause between 12,000 and 23,000 fatalities globally (IPCC 1996). One of the biggest death tolls from a natural disaster has been caused by tropical cyclones. For instance, a cyclone that hit Bangladesh in April 1991 caused more than 140,000 fatalities, displaced more than 10 million people, and caused $2 billion in damages. In November 1970, a similar storm claimed more than 250,000 lives.

In recent years, thousands of lives have also been lost in China, India, Thailand, and the Philippines (Southern 1992).

Nearly all of the recent hurricane damage growth occurred over a prolonged period of declining storm frequency and intensity (Landsea et al. 1996).

This indicates that fewer storms—which, on average, aren't any stronger than those from previous years—are to blame for the higher damages. It is the rapid population growth and development in exposed coastal areas that are mostly to blame for the rise in damages, not the number and intensity of storms.

CONCLUSION

The effects of hurricanes are now more likely to affect society. It is vital to view the pattern of rising losses during a time when hurricane frequency is often low as a serious warning. If no steps are done to lessen vulnerability, losses will inevitably rise to historic levels when hurricane frequencies and intensity reach levels seen earlier this century.

Residents of the U.S. Atlantic and Gulf Coasts are fortunate because hurricane watches and warnings, as well as shelters and well-planned evacuation routes, are easily accessible. This should not, however, lead to complacency because the hurricane issue cannot be deemed to be resolved (Pielke 1997).

Several disaster planning scenarios could occur here in the United States and cause a significant loss of life.

Consider a scenario in which traffic is gridlocked as evacuees attempt to leave the Florida Keys on the only open route. Or picture New Orleans, which is largely below sea level, taking the brunt of a strong hurricane that causes massive flooding in that low-lying metropolis. These kinds of situations necessitate an ongoing focus on lifesaving. It is impossible to say that the storm problem has been solved because it is always evolving as society does.